T0063077

The Israel Letters

*Words of Hope, Faith and Trust
Written with Love, Endorsed by Grace*

NANCY H. MONTGOMERY

WESTBOW°
PRESS
A DIVISION OF THOMAS NELSON
& ZONDERVAN

Scripture taken from the The Israel Bible, English
translation courtesy of the 1917 Jewish
Publication Society © Copyright by Israel365 and Teach for Israel;
36/18 Nachal Ein Gedi, Ramat Beit Shesmesh, Israel 99000,
www.TheIsraelBible.com. Used by permission. All rights reserved.

WestBow Press books may be ordered through booksellers or by contacting:

WestBow Press
A Division of Thomas Nelson & Zondervan
1663 Liberty Drive
Bloomington, IN 47403
www.westbowpress.com
1 (866) 928-1240

Because of the dynamic nature of the Internet, any web addresses or
links contained in this book may have changed since publication and
may no longer be valid. The views expressed in this work are solely those
of the author and do not necessarily reflect the views of the publisher,
and the publisher hereby disclaims any responsibility for them.

Any people depicted in stock imagery provided by Thinkstock are models,
and such images are being used for illustrative purposes only.
Certain stock imagery © Thinkstock.

ISBN: 978-1-4908-5227-0 (sc)
ISBN: 978-1-4908-5228-7 (e)

Library of Congress Control Number: 2014916543

Printed in the United States of America.

WestBow Press rev. date: 10/7/2014

This devotional is dedicated to today's Israel and members of Jewish and Christian communities throughout the world who daily express their love for her in prayer.

But thou, O LORD, shall endure forever; and thy remembrance unto all generations.

Thou shalt arise, and have mercy upon Zion: for the time to favour her, yea, the set time, is come.

Psalm 102:12-13
The Israel Bible

Contents

Foreword

The Israel Letters combines two of the most powerful tools in the world: prayer and the written Word. Whether your source of belief is drawn from the Tanakh or Old and New Testaments, your spirit will be stirred as you read the following pages. The author of this compact devotional is a woman whom God has given unmerited favor. In short, her testimony is comprised of a divine two-fold scheme: a vision and a calling.

The vision occurred more than 30 years ago, when Nancy was shown a map of the state of Ohio. On this map were eight dots, signifying eight key cities. Over time, Nancy learned that each of these cities would become locations for heavenly assignments. The interpretation of this vision remained hidden for some time. It was during this period, God began defining her calling. Using her talents and work in Christian radio, coupled with her activities in the Christian community, God began to morph her story into His'. Through these connections, Nancy was asked to serve as a Christian liaison to eight Jewish communities. The exact same ones revealed in the vision. It confirmed her assignment. Her mission, according to her earthly, as well as heavenly, commission, was to create a friendship between two strangers in Faith.

While Nancy no longer formally wears the hat of liaison, she continues to inspire others to stand fully in support of Israel and its people. This book serves as part of the proof.

Everything about this book is for God's Land and for His People.

What it boils down to is simply this: If you love God, you love Israel. And if you love Israel, the chances are good, you'll love this book. Everything about it brings praise to the Father. (Just what the author intended.) Its prayers of petition and proclamations of praise are meant for one purpose: To tell believers, Pray and Praise On!

"But thou art holy, O thou that inhabitest the praises of Israel..." Psalms 22:3 (KJV)

Liz Ridenour
fellow author and journalist

Preface

Encouraging understanding between Christians and Jews while supporting Israel is a wonderful calling. I find that if we can agree to disagree concerning our faiths God allows wonderful things to happen. When our working together seems a bit difficult or spiritual warfare rises to a higher level, I'm convinced God must chuckle. Many times during a radio broadcast a rabbi has remarked, "Nancy, the difference between us is we Jews expect the Messiah to come. You Christians expect Him to come back!" They are right. We do!

The Israel Letters were written during my prayer times. In Hebrew the word for eighteen is "chai" which means life. The letters are written to bring *life* into God's relationship with those who read them. Therefore I have included eighteen letters in this book.

Scripture references are included with each letter. All the Scriptures used come from the Tanakh (or Old Testament) portion of the Bible found in The Israel Bible[1] unless indicated. I hope your bible has excellent chain references and good footnotes. If it does, be sure to use them often. My faith grows by leaps and bounds when the Holy Spirit reveals God's hidden treasures tucked among the Scriptures. I have also included a prayer for today's Israel with each letter. I formatted this book to make it easier to take along wherever

---

[1]   The Israel Bible, English translation courtesy of the 1917 Jewish Publication Society © Copyright by Israel365 and Teach for Israel; 36/18 Nachal Ein Gedi, Ramat Beit Shesmesh, Israel 99000, www.TheIsraelBible.com

you go, making it convenient to stop and pray at any time. There are extra pages in the back of this devotional for notes, thoughts, extra scriptures or your special prayers to God for His beloved Israel.

A few months ago I wondered what I would include in this devotional when I started to write. When I penned the words "O Israel" writing began to flow, and each one of my prayer times became a new adventure with the Lord. Reading over what was written, I realized the words created a collection of short letters to Israel. The letters could have been written by a concerned brother or sister to their beloved sibling.

The Children of Israel receive God's grace throughout the Bible. If the word "grace" means only "the unmerited favor of God", its meaning is most apparent in Israel's repeated backsliding and God's repeated forgiveness of them. However the Hebrew understanding for grace is the word "chen" and includes God's *purpose* to establish a bond or relationship with His chosen people. Hence the author of the letters is called "Grace".

May the Holy One of Israel meet you in these pages. May He encourage you, strengthen you and pour out His grace upon you. Yes, *you*!

L'Chaim! - To Life!

Introduction

Summer 2014

O Friends,

We are friends, yes friends or haverim, of God when we love Him with all of our heart, all of our mind and all of our soul. Studying the Holy Bible reveals to us that Israel and the Jewish people hold a special place in salvation history for all the peoples of the world.

Recently I spent time with two friends – one a Christian and one a Jew. They had met through their love for Israel and the scriptures. They've had some adventures together over the years. Both love God deeply. They decided to agree to disagree about the tenets of their faiths and joined together to bless Israel. The Jewish friend put his arm around his Christian friend's shoulders and said, "Know what we've decided? We hope to be standing together in Israel when the Messiah comes. When He is near enough that we can speak to Him, we're going to ask Him if this is His *first* or *second* trip to The Land!"

God's word is a lamp to our feet and a guide to our paths. It was given to the Jews first then released to the Gentiles. Following its precepts give us life. God's precepts are sure to stand forever. Through them we rejoice! Day and night our voices join in praising Him, for His is our great joy. In our own ways, we worship Him, for He is holy. He brought back the Children of Israel to the Holy Land just as He promised. When she became a nation in 1948, Israel's population numbered 806,000. Now it numbers over 8,180,000[2]. Israel is a modern day wonder. She is God's statement to the world that His good trumps evil.

When I think of Israel's restoration as a nation, this passage of scripture comes to mind:

And say unto them, Thus saith the Lord GOD; Behold, I will take the children of Israel from among the heathen, whither they be gone, and will gather them on every side, and bring them into their own land: And I will make them one nation in the land upon the mountains of Israel; and one king shall be king to them all: and they shall be no more two nations, neither shall they be divided into two kingdoms any more at all. (Ezekiel 37:21-22)

This letter is written for Christians and Jews who have a heart to pray for Israel. Amongst us there is no wavering in our support for her. Israel is under pressure from without and from within. The enemy of her soul has reared his head under many ugly evil guises; terrorism and secularism being two of them. Times are difficult; anxiety and sorrows are great. Haters deny the Holocaust! The world tends to refuse to tell *Israel's* side of the story most of the time. Some of Israel's children *and their children* are squabbling over the right to settle the Land. Anti-Semitism is rising. Bombs explode in the skies above her.

Israelis are praying for their country, and so can we. Those who know God will love her and pray for her. Those who are convinced they know God but don't understand Israel

---

[2]   *Sources: Israeli Central Bureau of Statistics, 2014*

need to know *Him* better. There we have it - two ways to pray for Israel: pray to lift her up and pray for those who tear her down.

O My Friends, I am grateful you have picked up this book. If it seems good to you, I hope you will read it in those times when you are alone with God. Ask Him about the scriptures found here. Pray for our beloved Israel. Ask Him what you can do to help Israel NOW and *He* will tell you.

Blessed be the Holy One of Israel always…

Written with

His love,

Grace

Letter One

· ·

The Lord Preserved You

Zechariah 3:2; Isaiah 49:7-8; Psalm 23:3-5; Psalm 22:30-31

O Israel, the Righteous One, the Holy One of Israel, has preserved you! In an acceptable time He heard you. In the day of salvation He helped you. He has preserved you and kept you for Himself. Yes! Even when you walked in the valley of the shadow of death He was with you. From the ashes of the Holocaust He pulled you back as a brand from the fire. He said to the Enemy of your souls, "The Lord rebuke you, the Lord who has chosen Jerusalem, rebuke you!"

As Isaiah said:

Thus saith the LORD, In an acceptable time have I heard thee, and in a day of salvation have I helped thee: and I will preserve thee, and give thee for a covenant of the people, to establish the earth, to cause to inherit the desolate heritages. (Isaiah 49:8).

He comforts you with His words. He sighs with you in your grieving. He weeps with you as you weep. The Holy One restored you as a nation, O Israel. He desires to restore your soul and place you upon the path of righteousness. He longs to shower you with goodness and mercy. You are the posterity preserved to serve Him; making the way for the next generation to declare His righteousness to their children and their children's children.

Blessed be He,

Grace

Prayer:

Lord of Mercy, Great and Holy One, pour out Your Spirit of Compassion on Israel. They cannot see You, and yet they know You. They cannot touch Your face, but You can touch theirs. Wipe away their tears. Heal their great sorrows. Gather the fragments of this great people's soul and heal them. Restore them that they may turn completely to You, their Great and Mighty God, for You alone are their Redeemer. You are the Holy One of Israel, and we worship you.

Letter Two

* *

Love the LORD, Your God

Deuteronomy 30:15-20; Psalm 16; Isaiah 38:15-20

O Israel, love the LORD, Your God! Walk in His ways and keep His commandments. Set Him continually before you! Remember the words of King David. Consider Psalm 16. He wrote it and called it, "The Hope of the Faithful and the Messiah's Victory." He wrote this psalm because he understood these things. David had experienced an encounter with God, the Holy One of Israel! Make the words of this psalm personal and you will find that by setting the Lord continually before you, it is as if *He* is at your right hand all the time. You will know deep in your heart that He will not let you be shaken from The Land. This leads to a glad heart and rejoicing in your soul. King David's hope was inspired by faith in HIM.

King Hezekiah also had an encounter with the LORD, Your God. The great grace he received was so amazing that he wrote a song. He said, "The living man, he shall praise you, as I do this day; the father shall make known the truth to your children. The Lord was ready to save me!"

The LORD was ready to save me: therefore we will sing my songs to the stringed instruments all the days of our life in the house of the LORD (Isaiah 38:20)

3

O Israel, the Lord is at hand. Yes, He is close! Desire an encounter as David's. Pray for an encounter with HIM such as Hezekiah's. Let HIM be more special to you than the very land upon which you live!

Blessed be He,

Grace

Prayer:

Holy One, Holy Great and Mighty One, pour out your Spirit on Israel once again, we pray. Creator of our hearts, turn Israel's heart to You. Let them remember Your words. Remind them that above all they are to love You. Yes, love You; even more than their Land. Open their eyes and help them understand that one will not be without the other, as life is not sustained without breath. Prepare them, O Lord, prepare them for encounters with You. Move so deeply among them that the very face of their nation is changed. Yes, changed! Let the face of their nation glow like the face of Moses at the revelation of the Great and Mighty God. Let them say with once voice: "You are the Holy One of Israel and we worship You with all of our strength, with all of our heart, with all of our soul."

Letter Three

The Lord Will Raise Up Your Soldiers

Proverbs 16:3, 9; Psalm 89:11-23; Psalm 22:3

O Israel, the Lord will raise up your soldiers! And He will make them like the sword of a mighty man. Yes, your soldiers; your sons and your daughters. He who raises them up will defend them as they defend you. When the enemy comes in like a flood against you, the Spirit of the Lord will raise a standard against him.

So shall they fear the name of the LORD from the west, and his glory from the rising of the sun. When the enemy shall come in like a flood, the Spirit of the LORD shall lift up a standard against him. (Isaiah 59:19)

O Israel let your commanders commit their work to the Lord that their plans might be established by Him; then He will direct your steps. The Lord desires for His hand to be established over you so that neither your enemies nor the sons of wickedness are able to afflict you.

Even the G-d that executeth vengeance for me, and bringeth down peoples under me, And that bringeth me forth from mine enemies; yea, Thou liftest me up above them that rise up against me; Thou deliverest me from the violent man. (II Samuel 22:48-49)

5

Even in this day your soldiers stand in the plains and worship the Lord. He will move heaven and earth to fight for you!

Blessed be He,

Grace

Prayer:

Oh Mighty One, the soldiers of Israel rise with the sun and wrap Your words, Your promises, on their minds and tuck them into their hearts. When they turn to You and pray for their nation they face Jerusalem. O Great and Merciful One, send your Spirits of Might and Wisdom to strengthen them in the smallest of tasks and in the most monumental of assignments. Let Your Great Grace accompany them throughout the night and throughout the day. When the enemy of their souls tries to defeat them with fear and unbelief in You, let echoes of the songs of praise and deliverance spoken by their lips and hidden in their hearts each morning burst past his taunts. You inhabit the praises of Your people Israel. Their soldiers give you all glory, honor and praise, before their battles. O Holy One, answer them with Your great love.

Letter Four

• •

Trust in the Lord Forever

Isaiah 26:3-4; Psalm 9:10; Psalm 143:8

O Israel, trust in the Lord! As Isaiah said, "Trust in the Lord forever, for in YAH, the Lord, is your everlasting strength." Isaiah also shared a God precept important for you in every hour: the Lord will keep you in perfect peace when your mind is tuned into Him because *He knows* that you trust in Him. You will not be afraid of evil tidings if your heart is steadfast, trusting in the Holy One of Israel.

King Hezekiah was a great king. Those who wrote about him credited his greatness to his *trust* in the Lord. Consider some of the words concerning him found in the Book of Kings:

He trusted in the Lord God of Israel, so that after him was none like him among all the kings of Judah, nor who were before him. For he held fast to the Lord; he did not depart from following Him, but kept His commandments, which the Lord had commanded Moses. The Lord was with him; he prospered wherever he went. And he rebelled against the king of Assyria and did not serve him. He subdued the Philistines, as far as Gaza and its territory, from watchtower to fortified city. (2Kings 18:5-8 NKJ)

O Israel, you are His special nation. The Lord has brought you from the ends of the earth, and He is still gathering you! You will always need the Holy One's direction when involved in the affairs of men. Please remember this: when you trust in the Lord you can depend upon Him to direct your steps.

Blessed be He,

Grace

Prayer:

O Mighty One, pour out Your Spirit on Your people Israel yet again. Meet their trust with confirmations of Your great love and little wonders that lift up their souls. Lift them up so high that they become aware of Unbelief, the enemy of their souls, lurking around casting doubt on the truth of Who You Are – the One True God. Those who know Your name put their trust in You; for You, Lord, have not forsaken those who seek You.

Letter Five

· ·

It Is Time to Seek the Lord

Hosea 10:12, Amos 5:4, Proverbs 8:17, Jeremiah 50:4-5

O Israel, it is time to seek the Lord! Hosea spoke these words to your forefathers and he was absolutely right! His words are wisdom for you now. At another time Amos said by the Lord, "Seek me that you may live." There are those among you whose hearts are so damaged, so full of grief and fear, that they behave as fools and say there is no God in Israel. They are blinded to reality. Their blindness seeks to destroy you!

The LORD looked down from heaven upon the children of men, to see if there were any that did understand, and seek God.

Have all the workers of iniquity no knowledge? Who eat up my people as they eat bread, and call not upon the LORD.

There were they in great fear: for God is in the generation of the righteous. (Psalm 14:2, 4-5)

O Israel, the Lord loves those who love Him, and those who diligently seek Him. His love is your protection. Say to the

LORD, Your God, "We choose to be the generation of the righteous!"

Blessed be He,

Grace

Prayer:

Come O Holy One and pour out your Spirit upon the people of Israel! Encourage them in weaknesses and times of weeping to seek You. Remind them of Your words. Remind them that You love them, and that they are joined to You in a perpetual covenant which will not be forgotten. O Holy One, lift them up with Your everlasting arms. We adore You.

Letter Six

• •

You Have Found Grace in God's Sight

Exodus 33:1-23; Zechariah 12:10-14; Malachi 4:1-6

O Israel, you have found grace in God's sight. Yes, from your earliest days His grace has been with you. Consider Moses and the Children of Israel. Everyone agrees that getting all of the Israelites out of Egypt was an awesome act of God. When the Children of Israel arrived at Mt. Horeb, they were confronted with *being set free* in the wilderness.

If grace means only "the unmerited favor of God", their repeated backsliding and God's repeated forgiveness *of* them makes His grace towards the Children of Israel very apparent. Yet His amazing grace towards them goes deeper. It also includes God's *purpose* to establish an eternal relationship with the Jewish people.

When some of the Children of Israel made a golden calf and began to worship it, God could have destroyed all of them, yet He didn't. However, He did decide He would go no farther with them on the journey to the Promised Land; then Moses and God had a conversation:

"And he said unto Him: 'If Thy presences go not with me, carry us not up hence. For wherein now shall it be known that I have found grace in Thy sight, I and Thy people? Is it not in that

Thou goest with us, so that we are distinguished, I and Thy people, from all the people that are upon the face of the earth?'

And HaShem said unto Moses: 'I will do this thing also that thou hast spoken, for thou hast found grace in My sight, and I know thee by name." (Exodus 33:15-17)

O Israel, these are different times far away from the days of Moses, but not so far away from certain words of the prophets. Of course prophetic words have been up for debate since the day they were spoken. Yet of all the words spoken about grace, Zechariah shared *a special grace*. He said that the Almighty would send the Spirit of Grace and the Spirit of Supplication upon Israel one day. Blessed be the Holy One of Israel who extends His grace to you, O Israel!

Blessed be He,

Grace

Prayer:

O Holy One of Israel, Todah! Thank you for the miracle of today's Israel! Turn the eyes of Your people of faith throughout the nations towards Israel. Fill their hearts with the words of Your testimony concerning Israel Your beloved. Protect her cities. Come quickly with healing in Your wings and comfort the souls of her people. Turn the eyes of the fathers to the children and the eyes of the children to the fathers once again.

Letter Seven

• •

The Lord Will Save Your Children

Jeremiah 31:15; Isaiah 49:25, Psalm 24:1-6

O. *O Israel*, the Lord will save your children! Your years have not been easy. Like Rachel you weep for your children. When you cry out for your children the Lord hears you. Remember the Holy One of Israel who tells you He will contend with those who contend with you. He will save your children! O Israel be comforted, yes, comforted. God says your iniquity is pardoned, for surely you have received double for all of your sins.

Comfort ye, comfort ye my people, saith your God. Speak ye comfortably to Jerusalem, and cry unto her, that her warfare is accomplished, that her iniquity is pardoned: for she hath received of the LORD's hand double for all her sins. (Isaiah 40:1-2)

O Israel, you are tired. You are wearied by fighting and contention. You fear that your actions have put your sons and daughters in harm's way. But the Lord would encourage you! Remember the words of comfort and strategy He has given you. Mull over them. Read them out loud to your children.

Even the youths shall faint and be weary, and the young men shall utterly fall: But they that wait upon the LORD shall renew their strength; they shall mount up with wings as eagles; they shall run, and not be weary; and they shall walk, and not faint. (Isaiah 40:30-31)

O Israel be as Jacob! Be the generation that seeks the face of the LORD, Your God!

Blessed be He,

Grace

Prayer:

O Lord of Power and Grace, today's Israel is now over sixty-five years back in the Land. These You have gathered from the ends of the earth are the generations You chose to return. O Holy One, in the days of old they asked, "Who may ascend up to the hill of the Lord. Who may stand in Your holy place?" They have returned, O Lord, they wait for you. Show them Your ways, teach them Your paths. You are the God of their salvation. Let them turn their faces to You. Listen as they cry out for their children; for their descendants shall inherit the earth if they fear You. You will show your covenant to those who fear you. Pluck their feet from the mire that holds them back from worshipping You. Enlighten their minds with Your truths that they may rejoice in You. O Holy One of Israel, we bow in worship before You.

Letter Eight

• •

Our God is Awesome

Nehemiah 1:5; Deuteronomy 7:21; Psalm 68:35

O Israel, our God is awesome! He is the LORD, the God of Heaven, the great awesome God, who keeps His covenant of love with those who love him and keep His commandments. He has given you back the Land. You are modern day Israel; a true wonder and a sign of His favor. Remember when your forefathers heard Him speak from the mountain? They realized WHO He is; as has no generation since. Consider what He said about *that* generation:

"I have heard what this nation has to say. They have spoken well. If only their hearts would always remain this way, where they are in such awe of Me. They would then keep My commandments for all time, so that it would go well with them and their children forever."
(Deuteronomy 5:23-25 NKJ)

As for today's enemies, don't be terrified by them, for the LORD, Your God, who is among you is a great and awesome God.

Blessed be He,

Grace

15

Prayer:

O Mighty One, You are awesome in your sanctuary! You are the God of Israel who gives power and strength to Your people. O Holy One, pour out Your Spirit upon Israel once again. We will forever praise You!

$\mathscr{L}$etter $\mathscr{N}$ine

• •

Jerusalem is a Joy, and Her People a Gladness

Isaiah 65:18; Isaiah 30:19; Micah 4:2

$\mathscr{O}$ $\mathscr{I}$*srael*, Jerusalem is a joy, and her people a gladness. The Lord says your people shall dwell in Jerusalem. He says the time is coming when they shall weep no more for He intends to be gracious to them. The Lord will hear their cries and answer them. The Lord will defend Jerusalem!

As birds flying, so will the LORD of hosts defend Jerusalem; defending also he will deliver it; and passing over he will preserve it. (Isaiah 31:5)

O Israel, Jerusalem shall continue to be the Testimony of God. Those who love you say, "Come let us go up to the mountain of the Lord and to the house of the God of Jacob!" They love and delight in Jerusalem. Others are failing the test; they are stumbling badly when it comes to understanding the Mighty One's great love for Jerusalem. They refuse to recognize that it is *He* who gathered up the outcasts of Israel to build up Jerusalem. They plot against Him when they plot against you. They are drinking wine from the fruit of bad theology! They fail to hear the word of the Lord.

In that day shall the LORD defend the inhabitants of Jerusalem; and he that is feeble among them at that day

*shall be as David; and the house of David shall be as God,
as the angel of the LORD before them. And it shall come to
pass in that day, that I will seek to destroy all the nations
that come against Jerusalem. (Zechariah 12:8-9)*

Blessed be He,

Grace

Prayer:

O Holy One of Israel, open the eyes of those who fail to
recognize that it is You who set Jerusalem in the midst
of the nations and the countries around her. Woo them to
repentance before they are destroyed. Let all who love You,
O Mighty One, prosper because they choose NOW to pray
for the wellbeing of Israel and the peace of Jerusalem. For
the sake of Jerusalem and your people Israel, Holy One, we
come seeking their good. Let Your Spirit fall on Jerusalem
so all turn their faces up to You and cry, "Holy!" You are the
Holy One of Israel, and we worship You.

Letter Ten

• •

Let All the People Say Amen

Psalm 3:1-3; Psalm 106:48; Numbers 6:24-26

O Israel, let all the people say Amen! Even as you see many foes rising up against you, take courage from the knowledge of the Lord written in the scriptures. It belongs to you. Yes, you! Declare, "You, Mighty One, are a shield around me. You bestow glory upon me and lift up my head. Amen!"

Remember the prayer of King David toward the end of his forty year reign. He prayed with the assembly of all the people. David, a man after God's own heart prayed:

Blessed be thou, LORD God of Israel our father, for ever and ever.

Thine, O LORD is the greatness, and the power, and the glory, and the victory, and the majesty: for all that is in the heaven and in the earth is thine; thine is the kingdom, O LORD, and thou art exalted as head above all.

Both riches and honour come of thee, and thou reignest over all; and in thine hand is power and might; and in thine hand it is to make great, and to give strength unto all.

Now therefore, our God, we thank thee, and praise thy glorious name. (I Chronicles 29:10-13)

O Israel let all the people, say AMEN!

Blessed be He,

Grace

Prayer:

Father, for the wellbeing of Israel we now pray. May You pour out your Spirit on her sons and daughters. Bless and keep them; make Your face shine upon them, lift up Your countenance upon them, and give all Israel Your peace.

Letter Eleven

. . . .

No Longer Shall They Pull You Up

Hosea 2:23; Daniel 7:9

O *Israel*, the Lord has given you a future and a hope. He has planted you for Himself on your special piece of earth, never to be uprooted again! He saw the destruction against you by those who tried to put words in His mouth. They said, "Lo Ammi" or "You are not My people." Instead He said, "Ammi!" "You are My people!"

And I will bring again the captivity of my people of Israel, and they shall build the waste cities, and inhabit them; and they shall plant vineyards, and drink the wine thereof; they shall also make gardens, and eat the fruit of them.

And I will plant them upon their land, and they shall no more be pulled up out of their land which I have given them, saith the LORD thy God. (Amos 9:14-15)

The Ancient of Days remains the same forever. He raised up prophets to record His thoughts toward you. These words were given to your people and their kings, and they were not always welcomed. Nevertheless, His words have stood the test of time and are relevant for today!

For I know the thoughts that I think toward you, says the Lord, thoughts of peace and not of evil, to give you a future and a hope. (Jeremiah 29:11)

O Israel, who is like the Mighty One your Redeemer?

Blessed be He,

Grace

Prayer:

O Holy One, pour out Your Spirit on the inhabitants of Israel. Prepare them for their great future. Plant seeds of hope in their hearts to replace those now found there of sorrow and distress. Water the seeds with the tears of those who love and pray for them throughout the world; until the seeds of little hope become fields of beauty especially prepared for the coming of the great King. Let their cries of "Hosanna" echo throughout the earth as they unite with perfect hope for the glory due them. Long have they waited to hear Your voice once again. Lord of Glory, we worship You.

Letter Twelve

· ·

With the Lord There is Mercy

Psalm 118:1-4; Psalm 130:7; Leviticus 26:11

O Israel, give thanks to the Lord for His great mercy! Let Israel now say, "His mercy endures forever!" Remember the manna He dropped as dew every morning in the wilderness and how your forefathers were sent to collect it each day. Now you have no manna, but He brings you something greater. He brings you His great mercies. What is this mercy? It is God's *"chesed."* It is His steadfast, unfailing love for you. Yes, you! It is the same as His gift of grace; the unmerited favor He pours out on those who truly love Him.

O Israel, calamities come upon your nation without warning by those who are committed to seeing you destroyed. In spite of their hatred and taunts, the Lord God Almighty continues to bring your people home. How great is He!

From the earliest time in the history of your people, wise leaders have known victory comes from seeking Him. Even the smallest of His children can cry out for His mercy, and He will answer. Like a mother bird, He will give you refuge.

Be merciful unto me, O God, be merciful unto me: for my soul trusteth in thee: yea, in the shadow of thy wings will

23

I make my refuge, until these calamities be overpast. I will cry unto God most high; unto God that performeth all things for me. He shall send from heaven, and save me from the reproach of him that would swallow me up. Selah. God shall send forth his mercy and his truth. (Psalm 57:1-3)

The Lord broke the bands of the yoke you bore when you were dispersed among the nations. Now you, as a nation, choose to walk upright as His people. He tells you, "If you walk in My statutes and keep My commandments, and perform them, I will walk among you and be your God; and *you shall* be My people." With the LORD *there is mercy*, and with Him *is* abundant redemption. These are the truths that set you free.

Blessed be He,

Grace

Prayer:

God of Mercy, powerful and strong, pour out your Spirit on Your people Israel. Calamities are piling up, waiting to happen in her midst, but You are the Great and Mighty One who promises to be in her midst if she is faithful. O Holy One, shower her people with new mercies every morning, every evening, throughout the day. Confound her enemies. Stop them in their tracks. And although it would seem impossible to man, make your intervention so known to her enemies that it is as clear as if You left your calling card: *Commander of the Heavenly Hosts*. Lord, may those enemies, stymied in their wicked plans, realize Your good trumps their evil and turn instead to You. For nothing is impossible with you, Holy One of Israel!

Letter Thirteen

Receive Your Promises

Genesis 1: 2; Ezekiel 11:16-20; Isaiah 43:1-18; Psalm 90:1

O Israel, receive your promises! For they are many. Draw aside and search the Holy writings. Gather your promises around you. Make up your mind to receive all He desires to give you!

But Zion said, The LORD hath forsaken me, and my Lord hath forgotten me. Can a woman forget her sucking child, that she should not have compassion on the son of her womb? yea, they may forget, yet will I not forget thee. (Isaiah 49:14-15)

Receive the one heart the Lord has promised to your nation. Yes to you! He has promised you a unity of hearts so that He can place a new spirit within you. Has your heart become stony because of your great trials? It is a stony heart that leaves you comfortless. He will bring comfort to you as a child. Rejoice in your promises of old, O Israel, for they remain for you now. He has given you back your Land. He has established the work of your hands.

Return, O LORD! How long? And have compassion on Your servants. Oh, satisfy us early with Your mercy, That we may rejoice and be glad all our days! Make us glad according to

26

the days in which You have afflicted us, The years in which we have seen evil.

Let Your work appear to Your servants, And Your glory to their children. And let the beauty of the LORD our God be upon us,

And establish the work of our hands for us; Yes, establish the work of our hands. (Psalm 90:13-17 NKJ)

He returned you from captivity. O Israel, remember and receive His promises for you are His people. He desires to be your one true God. He has been your dwelling place for all generations.

Blessed be He,

Grace

Prayer:

O Lord, You are El Shadai, God Almighty and nothing is too difficult for You! Pour out your Spirit on the people of Israel. Shower them with Your love and comfort; free them from fear and anxiety. Let them remember and rejoice in the many promises you have kept for them; for the many promises You are ready to fulfill. Cause great excitement to rise in their midst as they begin to perceive Your great Glory once again.

• •

You Are a Banner to the Nations

Psalm 107:2-3; Exodus 17:8-16

O Israel, you are a banner to the nations! The world watches as the Holy One continues to increase and prosper you in front of your enemies. You are the redeemed of the Lord! He gathered you out of their lands. He is gathering you still. He brings back your children. And yet even now your soul melts because of trouble and you are at wit's end.

They that go down to the sea in ships, that do business in great waters; These see the works of the LORD, and his wonders in the deep. For he commandeth, and raiseth the stormy wind, which lifteth up the waves thereof. They mount up to the heaven, they go down again to the depths: their soul is melted because of trouble. They reel to and fro, and stagger like a drunken man, and are at their wit's end. Then they cry unto the LORD in their trouble, and he bringeth them out of their distresses. (Psalm 107:23-28)

You are just as He said: a banner for the nations! In you He is assembling the outcasts of Israel, and gathering together the dispersed of Judah from the four corners of the Earth.

And it shall come to pass in that day, that the Lord shall set his hand again the second time to recover the remnant of his people, which shall be left... And he shall set up an ensign for the nations, and shall assemble the outcasts of Israel, and gather together the dispersed of Judah from the four corners of the earth. (Isaiah 11:11-12)

This is no time to be faint hearted. This is no time to lose your resolve to keep all that He has given you!

Blessed be He,

Grace

Prayer:

O Holy One of Israel, pour out your Spirit on Israel once again! Send out a call to her friends throughout the world. Call forth those who are like Aaron and Hur. Men and women with a Spirit of Might who gather from a distance in prayer to hold up Israel's arms as battles in heaven and earth continue to rage around her. O Glorious One, You know who these prayer warriors are. They are worshippers of You. Let them continue in prayer around the clock. Undergird with strength from heaven those who come in "ships" to help Israel, bringing her gifts of help and comfort and steadfast prayer. We will rally to Your banner, O Holy One of Israel! You are our God! We worship you.

• •

The Lord's Faithfulness Will Not Fail You

Psalm 55:1-5; Psalm 22:3-6

O *Israel,* the Lord keeps His word! In spite of your wanderings and backslidings, the Lord has promised that He will not take away His kindness towards you or let His faithfulness fail. He says He won't break His covenant with you or alter the words He has spoken. He has sworn this by His holiness.

Nevertheless my lovingkindness will I not utterly take from him, nor suffer my faithfulness to fail. My covenant will I not break, nor alter the thing that is gone out of my lips. Once have I sworn by my holiness that I will not lie unto David. (Psalm 89:33-35)

Be aware always that He is aware. He is aware of the state of your nation. He knows your perils from without, and He knows your perils from within. He knows that in this very hour you are like the words of a psalm:

Give ear to my prayer, O God; and hide not thyself from my supplication. Attend unto me, and hear me: I mourn in my complaint, and make a noise; Because of the voice of the enemy, because of the oppression of the wicked: for they cast iniquity upon me, and in wrath they hate me. (Psalm 55:2-3)

O Israel, the Lord told you to cast your burdens on *Him*, He wants to sustain you. Walk in His counsel. He won't allow the righteous to be moved. *He desires to renew a right spirit in you.* Yes, you!

Blessed be He,

Grace

Prayer:

O Mighty God, pour out your Spirit on Israel once again. Set the peoples' spirits free causing them to dance before You as David danced; to sing as David sang; to praise as David praised! For you, O Mighty One, inhabit the praises of Your people. Break all of their barriers! Let praise become spontaneous. Cause it to bubble up within them. Let them raise such a ruckus that the glass ceiling of oppression over their nation is broken as You send *Your Great Glory* down upon them. O Mighty One, restore to them the joy of their salvation and renew a right Spirit within them. Todah, Mighty One. Todah! Thank you! Thank you!

Letter Sixteen

. . . .

The Lord Has Given You His Great Treasure

Isaiah 33; Psalm 23:3

O Israel, the Lord has given you precious gifts! Wisdom and knowledge are jewels stored within His words. The fear of the Lord is your wisdom.

The LORD is exalted; for he dwelleth on high: he hath filled Zion with judgment and righteousness. And wisdom and knowledge shall be the stability of thy times, and strength of salvation: The fear of the LORD is his treasure. (Isaiah 33:5-6)

This knowledge is the true treasure He has given to you. Yes, you! Indeed His words are wrapped in the Holy Scriptures and are the very treasures that serve as lamps to your feet and lights for your path. They lead you to salvation. Yet many in Israel have strayed! If only they knew HIM. They would understand He *really* is omnipotent. His words may have been written thousands of years before they were born, but not before He knew those who strayed would need them!

The prophet Hosea warned,

My people are destroyed for lack of knowledge: because thou hast rejected knowledge, I will also reject thee, that thou shalt be no priest to me: seeing thou hast forgotten the law of thy God, I will also forget thy children. (Hosea 4:6)

O Israel, come before the Lord with outstretched arms this day and ask Him to draw back the ones among your people who have turned away; the ones being destroyed for lack of knowledge; the ones who refuse His great treasure and have no fear.

Blessed be He,

Grace

Prayer:

We beseech you, O Mighty One, to send your Spirit once more to Israel. Bring those who rebel against You, who refuse You now, back into Your flock. You are their Shepard, O Holy One. You are the lover of their souls. It is You who can lead them in the paths of righteousness. For Your Name's sake, O Holy One of Israel, do a new thing in them. Restore their souls. Todah! We thank you, O Holy One. We adore you. You are the Shepard of our souls.

Letter Seventeen

O Israel Proclaim, "The-Lord-Is-My-Banner"

Psalm 95; Exodus 17:1-7, 14-16

O Israel, consider the day when Moses built an altar and named it The-Lord-is-My-Banner. Yes, consider the first time He revealed Himself to you by this name! You were just becoming a new nation then when your forefathers fought against Amalek; when a tribe descended from Esau came upon you. They arrived and attacked leaving Moses no choice but to call up the troops - such as they were - and engage the Amalekites in battle.

And Moses said unto Joshua: 'Choose us out men, and go out, fight with Amalek; tomorrow I will stand on the top of the hill with the rod of G-d in my hand.' So Joshua did as Moses had said to him, and fought with Amalek; and Moses, Aaron, and Hur went up to the top of the hill. And it came to pass, when Moses held up his hand, that Israel prevailed; and when he let down his hand, Amalek prevailed. But Moses' hands were heavy; and they took a stone, and put it under him, and he sat thereon; and Aaron and Hur stayed up his hands, the one on the one side, and the other on the other side; and his hands were steady until the going down of the sun. And Joshua discomfited Amalek and his people with the edge of the sword. (Exodus 17:9-13)

O Israel there are disturbances both on the ground and in the spiritual realm. War with the modern Amalekites is upon you in the physical reality; and so it is in the spiritual atmosphere all around you. Once more they declare war upon you and upon the One True God.

Then the Lord said to Moses, "Write this for a memorial in the book and recount it in the hearing of Joshua that I will utterly blot out the remembrance of Amalek from under heaven." And Moses built an altar and called its name, The-Lord-Is-My-Banner; for he said, "Because the Lord has sworn: the Lord will have war with Amalek from generation to generation." (Exodus 17:14-16)

Call for people of prayer to assemble alongside you for the Lord is your banner. Let their prayers hold up the arms of your soldiers around the clock. God is at war with the spirit of Amalek for all generations, and *He will prevail*; as will you. Yes, you!

Blessed be He,

Grace

Prayer:

O Holy One, thank you for placing your banner over today's Israel! Thank you for raising up Jews and Christians all over the world to be to Israel as Aaron on one side and Hur on the other. Open the eyes of Israel's friends in churches and synagogues all over the world to the reality of today's battles. Impel them to seek Your Face concerning Israel's foes. Reveal the true identity - the real face - of those warring against Israel. O Mighty One, send all forms of help to Israel. Pour out your Spirit on Israel. Holy One of Israel, we worship you.

Letter Eighteen

• •

Be of Good Courage

Psalm 27:11-14; Numbers 22:2-24:25; Psalm 34:7

O *Israel*, be of good courage! Turn your face to God, and He will strengthen your heart. He will not deliver you to the will of your adversaries. He reminds you day by day in your Torah portions of His steadfast commitment to you. Remember Balak and Balaam in the Book of Numbers! Read past the verses about Balaam's donkey and grasp the truths embedded in the words. Repeatedly Balak asked Balaam to seek God to curse you and every time God blessed you. God gave Balaam an insight to tell your enemy:

G-d is not a man, that He should lie; neither the son of man, that He should repent: when He hath said, will He not do it? or when He hath spoken, will He not make it good? Behold, I am bidden to bless; and when He hath blessed, I cannot call it back. (Numbers 23:19-29)

O Israel, the Lord is still with you! You have the Great King's friendship. Balaam prophesied saying, *"Since God brought them out of Egypt, they are like His highest expression of strength."(Numbers 23:22 NKJ)*

Your history since He brought you back to the Land has been the same. This you know: the Angel of the Lord encamps all around those who fear Him, and delivers them. Blessed is the man who trusts in Him! Wait on the Lord; be of good courage and He shall strengthen your heart.

Blessed be He,

Grace

Prayer:

O Mighty God, in this hour teach Israel Your way. Lead them in a smooth path because of their enemies. Do not deliver them to the will of their foes. False witnesses rise against them and breathe out violence. O Holy One, let your love flow to them from the ends of the earth from those who love You. Speak gently to Israeli hearts where only You can enter saying, "Don't lose heart. I know you believe in Me. I desire for you to see My goodness to you in the land of the living." Todah! Thank You, O Mighty One! We are devoted to you.

Prayer Notes ❧ *Letter One*

. . . .

Prayer Notes ❦ *Letter Three*

. . . .

Prayer Notes ❧ *Letter Five*

Prayer Notes ～ *Letter Seven*

Prayer Notes ∽ *Letter Thirteen*

· ·

Prayer Notes ❧ Letter Fifteen

. . . .

Prayer Notes ∞ *Letter Seventeen*

. . . .

About the Author

Nancy Montgomery is the founder of Haverim, a non-profit organization created to educate concerning today's Israel and encourage understanding between Christians and Jews. The name of the organization is a Hebrew word for friends. Nancy's expertise in Jewish/Christian relations dates back to her early days in radio. She was asked by a local Christian radio station to host a weekly one hour broadcast focused on her great love for Israel and the Jewish people. That radio program sparked a long standing friendship between Nancy and Jewish communities throughout Ohio. Nancy continued as a volunteer with local Christian radio for many years before becoming an independent radio program producer. Her radio program "Haverim" aired across Ohio, numerous states and as far away as Australia.

Nancy Montgomery has served in leadership capacities in her own church and numerous national organizations including leadership teams for Aglow International, President of the Columbus Diocesan Council of Catholic Women - the National Council of Catholic Women, and on the advisory board of Voices United for Israel in the early years before it became known as the Unity Coalition for Israel. She is a past member of the National Religious Broadcasters. She is also a friend and supporter of many like-minded Christian and Jewish organizations.

Nancy lives in Zanesville, Ohio with husband Tom and a very large Himalayan cat named Hank. *The Israel Letters* is her first book.

Nancy Montgomery can be contacted through her publisher or at Haverim's website: www.haverim.org

Haverim.org combines years of Christian-Jewish relations and Christian radio broadcasting to create a website committed to encouraging friendship and understanding between Christians and Jews. Together we support and bless today's Israel. www.haverim.org

Israel365 promotes the beauty and religious significance of Israel. Featuring the stunning photographs of more than 30 award winning Israeli photographers alongside an inspiring Biblical verse, Israel365 connects you with Israel each day. Israel 365 is also where you can learn more about *The Israel Bible* used as a resource for scriptures in this book. www.israel365.com

Breaking Israel News offers a fresh and biblical perspective on the latest news from Israel and the Middle East. Their bias is neither liberal nor conservative—just biblical. Breaking Israel News was started in July 2013, by Rabbi Tuly Weisz, founder and director of Israel365. The rabbi created the service in response to the requests he was getting from thousands of Jewish and Christian Zionists, who were interested in receiving more news and insight from Israel. On shoestring budget, and within this short time, the site has grown tremendously. Breaking Israel News is visited by thousands of people every day and 100,000 unique visitors over the course of a month from over 100 countries around the world. www.breakingisraelnews.com

Rather you are an old or a new friend of Israel, these new online resources will truly encourage you in your times of prayer for Israel. Nancy Montgomery